Life Skills

Taking Care of Your Body

by Emma Huddleston

FOCUS READERS®

PIONEER

www.focusreaders.com

Focus Readers is distributed by North Star Editions:
sales@northstareditions.com | 888-417-0195

Produced for Focus Readers by Red Line Editorial.

Photographs ©: Shutterstock Images, cover, 1, 8, 15 (food); iStockphoto, 4, 7, 11, 12, 15 (plate), 16, 19; Red Line Editorial, 21

Library of Congress Cataloging-in-Publication Data
Names: Huddleston, Emma, author.
Title: Taking care of your body / by Emma Huddleston.
Description: Lake Elmo, MN : Focus Readers, [2021] | Series: Life skills |
   Includes index. | Audience: Grades 2-3
Identifiers: LCCN 2020003397 (print) | LCCN 2020003398 (ebook) | ISBN
   9781644933473 (hardcover) | ISBN 9781644934234 (paperback) | ISBN
   9781644935750 (ebook pdf) | ISBN 9781644934999 (hosted ebook)
Subjects: LCSH: Hygiene--Juvenile literature.
Classification: LCC RA777 .H816 2021 (print) | LCC RA777 (ebook) | DDC
   613--dc23
LC record available at https://lccn.loc.gov/2020003397
LC ebook record available at https://lccn.loc.gov/2020003398

Printed in the United States of America
Mankato, MN
082020

About the Author

Emma Huddleston lives in the Twin Cities with her husband. She enjoys writing children's books and reading novels.

Table of Contents

Chapter 1

Caring for Your Body

All people must take care of their own bodies. People stay clean. They eat well. They also exercise.

People **sense** the world through their bodies. Their bodies let them run, jump, and play. People feel good when they take care of their bodies.

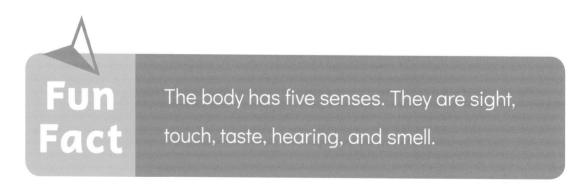

Fun Fact

The body has five senses. They are sight, touch, taste, hearing, and smell.

Chapter 2

Staying Clean

Germs can cause people to get sick. People wash their bodies to get rid of germs. People use soap. They take showers or baths.

People should brush their teeth two times every day. Brushing keeps teeth healthy. Also, people should wash their hands often. They should wash before eating. They should wash after using the bathroom.

Fun Fact

Flossing helps clean between teeth.

Chapter 3

Eating and Drinking

Eating healthy foods gives people energy. People need energy to move. Healthy foods also have **nutrients** that help bodies grow.

A **balanced** meal has food from more than one food group. Healthy foods include fruits, vegetables, and grains. Some people also eat **lean** meat.

People should drink lots of water. Bodies need water to work. People can also drink milk for its nutrients. There are many kinds of milk.

My Plate

My Plate shows what a balanced meal might look like.
It includes foods from all the different food groups.

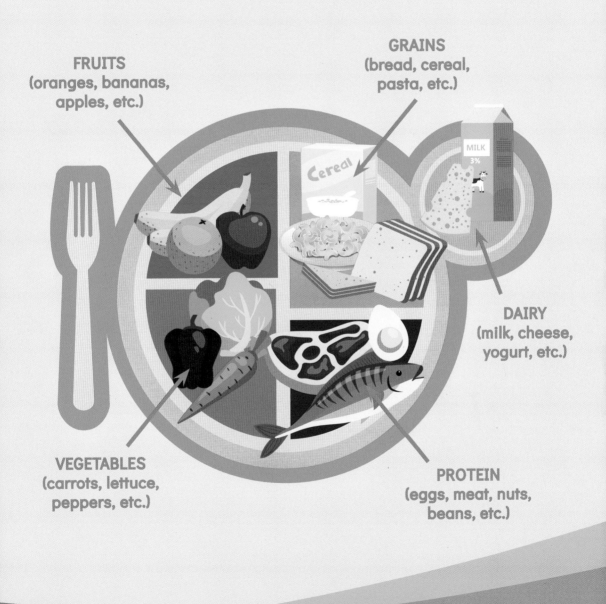

FRUITS
(oranges, bananas,
apples, etc.)

GRAINS
(bread, cereal,
pasta, etc.)

DAIRY
(milk, cheese,
yogurt, etc.)

VEGETABLES
(carrots, lettuce,
peppers, etc.)

PROTEIN
(eggs, meat, nuts,
beans, etc.)

Chapter 4

Exercising and Sleeping

Exercising means being active and moving your body. Exercise keeps muscles and bones strong. It can also be fun.

People should move their bodies every day. They can play sports or go on walks. They can swim, dance, or run. Rest is also important. Good sleep gives people energy for the next day.

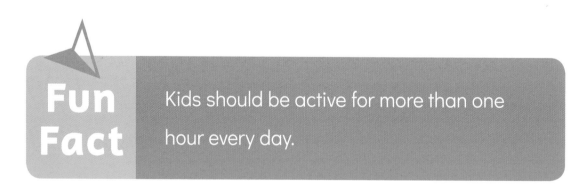

Fun Fact

Kids should be active for more than one hour every day.

Make a Routine

Many people follow a **routine** to stay healthy. Here is a sample routine for taking care of your body. You can create your own healthy routine. Think of ways you can stay clean, eat well, and exercise.

Morning	Afternoon	Evening
Wash: • Brush hair • Brush teeth • Wash hands before breakfast • Wash hands after using the bathroom	*Wash:* • Wash hands before lunch • Wash hands after using the bathroom	*Wash:* • Wash hands before dinner • Wash hands after using the bathroom • Shower or bathe • Brush teeth • Floss teeth
Eat: • Drink some kind of milk with breakfast	*Eat:* • Have fruit for a snack • Don't forget water!	*Eat:* • Eat vegetables with dinner
Move: • Walk dog	*Move:* • Help with chores • Play tag • Go to sports practice	*Move:* • Ride a bike

FOCUS ON

Taking Care of Your Body

Write your answers on a separate piece of paper.

1. Write a paragraph about how you can take care of your body.

2. What types of exercise do you enjoy? Why do you enjoy them?

3. Why is staying clean part of a healthy routine?
   A. It helps people stay active.
   B. It helps get rid of germs.
   C. It gives people energy.

4. Which of these options is an example of a healthy, balanced meal?
   A. a meal with only grains
   B. a meal with fruit and dessert
   C. a meal with vegetables, lean meat, and grains

Answer key on page 24.

Glossary

balanced
Having a mix of different items.

flossing
Using a thin string to clean between teeth.

germs
Tiny living things that can cause illness.

lean
Having little or no fat.

nutrients
Things that people, animals, and plants need to stay healthy.

routine
A set of actions someone does regularly.

sense
To take in information about the world.

To Learn More

BOOKS

Raij, Emily. *My Immune System: A 4D Book*.
North Mankato, MN: Capstone Publishing, 2019.

Sjonger, Rebecca. *On a Mission for Good Nutrition!*
New York: Crabtree Publishing Company, 2016.

NOTE TO EDUCATORS

Visit **www.focusreaders.com** to find lesson plans, activities, links, and other resources related to this title.

Index

Answer Key: 1. Answers will vary; **2.** Answers will vary; **3.** B; **4.** C